WRITING WARM-UPS

7–12

by

Lori Mammen

Printed in the U.S.A.

Also available:

WRITING WARM-UPS, K-6

Inquire at your local school supply store, or contact:

ECS Learning Systems, Inc.
P.O. Box 791437
San Antonio, Texas 78279-1437
1-800-68-TEACH

First Printing: December, 1989
Second Printing: June, 1991
Third Printing: February, 1993

ISBN 0-944459-08-0

Introduction

WHAT?   What are Writing Warm-Ups? They are brief and creative writing activities for teachers who want students to make the most of every minute in the classroom. Presented in simple, easy-to-use format, Warm-Ups are quick, convenient writing exercises that encourage students to enjoy and play with words. The activities motivate students to generate numerous and varied ideas. They challenge students to write creatively about a variety of topics.

HOW?   Warm-Ups can fit into any classroom. They can be used at the beginning of class to spark interest. The activities are also useful as stimuli for journal entries. Although Writing Warm-Ups usually require only a few minutes to complete, many of them can lead to longer, more developed pieces of writing as suggested in the extension section. You have many options for using Warm-Ups effectively in your classroom.

WHO?   Although most of the Warm-Ups are simple enough for young or beginning writers, they still require creative attention and are, therefore, appealing to these inexperienced writers. For very young writers the exercises can generate oral language. You can transcribe student responses onto charts, chalkboard, or paper. However, even very young students should have the opportunity to write their own responses as soon as possible. If you allow for "invented spellings," then young students can be writing on their own almost from the beginning.

Writing Warm-Ups are also for the older or more experienced student writers. The activities are just as appealing to this group of students. However, many of the warm-ups will lead to longer, more complex pieces of writing by these more mature writers.

The age and experience level of your students will determine the length, maturity, and complexity of their responses to the Writing Warm-Ups. However, the most important result of these activities will be student involvement in writing.

WHEN?   Because the Warm-Ups are brief, you can use them almost anytime during the teaching day. As the name implies, they provide a good "warm-up" at the beginning of class. They also provide worthwhile activities for the minutes that are often "lost" when the you are involved in taking attendance, sending messages, talking with individual students, or other such tasks. Some Warm-Ups offer excellent foundations for longer, more complete writing assignments, also. In fact, since each Warm-Up is classified according to the type of writing it might generate, you will find that many of the Warm-Ups merge nicely with your regular composition curriculum. No doubt, you will find many other times when Writing Warm-Ups fit into your teaching schedule.

When can Writing Warm-Ups be used in your classroom? You will find many appropriate times. When is the **most** appropriate time? Why not give Warm-Ups a try in your classroom **NOW**?

Using Writing Warm-Ups

You will find that all of the Writing Warm-Ups follow the same format and are, therefore, easy to follow. Once you are familiar with the basic pattern, you will be able to use them most effectively. Some Warm-Ups will serve only as motivators, while others will lead to more complete pieces of writing. You will be able to select the particular Warm-Ups most appropriate for your students. You will also be able to select the length of time and work your students will spend on each of the activities. The format is flexible enough to accommodate a variety of classroom situations. The next few pages explain how the Warm-Ups appear and offer suggestions about using them in your classroom. Read over this information before you begin using the activities with your students.

Format

All Writing Warm-Ups follow the same format. Once you are familiar with this outline, you will be able to use all or part of the activities successfully in your classroom.

Warm-Up: Each activity begins with a specific Writing Warm-Up. The Warm-Up will ask students to write about a specific question, problem, situation, etc. The writing stimulus will almost always challenge the student to think and write in a different, creative way. Most students will probably spend only 10-15 minutes to respond to the stimulus . (This will depend upon the age, grade, and maturity level of the students.) However, the thinking and creativity which occur during this brief time are of unquestionable value in developing student writing ability.

Purpose: All writing is done to communicate. However, a specific purpose (expressive, informative, persuasive) accompanies each Writing Warm-Up. When responding to the Warm-Up, students will *probably* write a response which is related to the specified purpose. You should **not** penalize students if their writing does not match the purpose listed with the Warm-Up. Use the listed purpose as a guide in selecting appropriate activities for your students. For example, if your students are learning informative writing as part of the writing curriculum, you might choose Warm-Ups classified as informative. These Warm-Ups will require students to practice a skill, or skills, related to that purpose. (See the section on Purposes for Writing for further information.)

| **Mode:** | Writers choose a variety of methods to achieve their purpose for writing. These methods are sometimes called the modes of writing. A specific mode (description, narration, classification) accompanies each Writing Warm-Up. Again, students will *probably* write a response which is related to the specified mode. However, you should **not** penalize students if their writing does not match the mode listed with the Warm-Up. Use the listed modes in the same way you use the listed purposes - as a guide for selecting appropriate activities for your students. (See the section on Modes of Writing for further information.) |

Creative Thinking Skills: All writing is creative. Creativity, however, entails a variety of specific thinking skills. The specific creative thinking skills (fluency, flexibility, originality, elaboration) necessary to respond effectively to each Warm-Up are listed with the activity. (See the section on Creative Thinking Skills for further information.)

Extension: A suggestion for a further writing/creative activity accompanies each Writing Warm-Up. The extension provides an opportunity for further student writing. Since these extensions require more time, you will want to select those most appropriate for your students according to your time and curriculum constraints. Some students may be interested in completing these activities independently. The extensions are always optional.

Teacher Notes/ Comments: This section is provided for you to take note of special interest a class or student shows for a particular assignment. You might also use the comment section to make note of changes you made which enhanced/extended the activity. Use this space in a way most beneficial to you and your students.

Purposes for Writing

Although there are many ways to categorize and describe the purposes for writing, the purposes used for the Writing Warm-Ups are those developed by James L. Kinneavy in *A Theory of Discourse* (Englewood Cliffs: Prentice-Hall, Inc. , 1971). In this text, Kinneavy lists four purposes for writing. **Informative** writing uses language to explore questions, provide information and produce evidence for certain questions. **Persuasive** writing uses language to try and change the thinking or attitudes of others. **Expressive** writing uses language to help the writer express personal feelings, thoughts, and ideas both as an outlet for these feelings and thoughts and as a way to make them clear to others. **Literary** writing uses language to provide pleasure for the reader and the writer. (Literary writing is not addressed in WRITING WARM-UPS.) While there are many ways to categorize the purposes for writing, Kinneavy's system is basically simple and easy to understand. While Warm-Ups may not be complete writing assignments, students must do certain kinds of thinking in order to respond to them. The skills they use will probably be related to the purpose which is listed with the activity.

Modes of Writing

As with the purposes for writing, there are several ways of categorizing the methods, or modes, a writer uses to achieve his/her purpose. The modes used for the Writing Warm-Ups are those developed by James L. Kinneavy in *A Theory of Discourse* (Englewood Cliffs: Prentice-Hall, Inc., 1971). He lists four modes of writing. **Descriptive** writing creates a clear picture of a scene, person, place, object or situation for the reader. **Narrative** writing relates a story or other material in chronological (time) order. **Classificatory** writing provides clear information by comparing objects, situations, people, etc. **Evaluative** writing refers to drawing a conclusion or making a judgment about some idea or situation. (Evaluation is not addressed in WRITING WARM-UPS.) Again, there are other systems for classifying the methods a writer uses to achieve his/her purpose, but Kinneavy's model offers a simple classification. Students will use certain kinds of thinking in order to respond to the Warm-Ups. The thinking skills they use will probably relate to the mode which is listed with each activity.

Creative Thinking Skills

Writing is a creative act, and it requires students to make use of the thinking skills necessary for any creative endeavor. Writing Warm-Ups address one or more of four creative thinking skills. **Fluency** is the ability to produce a large quantity of ideas, answers, or solutions. Fluency is a necessary writing skill since writers need a large storehouse of ideas for their writing. **Flexibility** is the ability to produce many different kinds of ideas, answers, or solutions. This skill allows the writer to view subjects from a different perspective and enhances his/her writing. **Originality** is the ability to produce unique and unusual ideas, answers, or solutions. Originality in writing helps give a piece a fresh and different approach or direction. **Elaboration** is the ability to provide new and meaningful details to ideas, answers, or solutions. Elaboration makes writing come alive because it helps the reader see a total picture. Fluency, flexibility, originality, and elaboration are all necessary to create effective pieces of writing. The Warm-Ups provide students with opportunities to practice these skills. With enough meaningful practice, students will begin to apply these important thinking skills to the other writing they do.

WARM-UP ONE

WARM-UP: Write a conversation a pencil and a book
might have at school.

PURPOSE: Expressive

MODE: Narrative

**CREATIVE
THINKING SKILLS:**   Flexibility, originality, elaboration

EXTENSION: It might be fun to perform this conversation
as a short play for your class. Write the
conversation in play form. Make a costume
for each of the characters.

**TEACHER NOTES/
COMMENTS:**

WARM-UP TWO

<table>
<tr><td>WARM-UP:</td><td>Which color is most like you? Explain why you think this color is like you.</td></tr>
<tr><td>PURPOSE:</td><td>Expressive</td></tr>
<tr><td>MODE:</td><td>Descriptive</td></tr>
<tr><td>CREATIVE THINKING SKILLS:</td><td>Flexibility, originality, elaboration</td></tr>
<tr><td>EXTENSION:</td><td>Write a poem based on the ideas you wrote in answer to the warm-up. Create a picture, painting, or other visual interpretation of the poem.</td></tr>
<tr><td>TEACHER NOTES/ COMMENTS:</td><td></td></tr>
</table>

WARM-UP THREE

WARM-UP: Would you rather be the wind or the rain? Explain the reason for your choice.

PURPOSE: Persuasive

MODE: Classificatory

CREATIVE THINKING SKILLS: Flexibility, originality, elaboration

EXTENSION: Write a fable that includes either the wind or the rain as the main character. What lesson will you try to teach in the fable?

TEACHER NOTES/ COMMENTS:

WARM-UP FOUR

WARM-UP: What is your favorite school subject? Explain why it is your choice.

PURPOSE: Persuasive

MODE: Descriptive

CREATIVE THINKING SKILLS: Originality, elaboration

EXTENSION: Create an advertisement for your favorite school subject. Design your advertisement to interest other students to take the same course.

TEACHER NOTES/ COMMENTS:

WARM-UP FIVE

WARM-UP: Write an apology for something you wish you had not done. Make your apology sincere.

PURPOSE: Expressive

MODE: Descriptive

CREATIVE THINKING SKILLS: Originality, elaboration

EXTENSION: Write an editorial titled one of the following: "It Is Always Important To Apologize" or "It Is Not Always Important To Apologize."

TEACHER NOTES/ COMMENTS:

WARM-UP SIX

WARM-UP: What three important tips would you offer someone for success in school?

PURPOSE: Informative

MODE: Narrative

CREATIVE THINKING SKILLS: Originality, elaboration

EXTENSION: Create a small pamphlet or flier titled "Success in School." In this pamphlet or flier, offer suggestions for succeeding in school.

TEACHER NOTES/ COMMENTS:

WARM-UP: Think of your favorite food. Can you describe it without giving its name?

PURPOSE: Informative

MODE: Descriptive

CREATIVE THINKING SKILLS: Flexibility, originality, elaboration

EXTENSION: Write a new recipe that includes your favorite food as one of the ingredients. Then write a description of it that would convince others to eat it.

TEACHER NOTES/ COMMENTS:

WARM-UP EIGHT

WARM-UP: You've been hired as a writer for a Chinese restaurant. Write two fortunes for the cookies.

PURPOSE: Informative

MODE: Narrative

CREATIVE THINKING SKILLS: Flexibility, originality

EXTENSION: Study the horoscope section in the newspaper. These columns follow a special style. Write original horoscopes. Write them in the same style.

TEACHER NOTES/ COMMENTS:

WARM-UP: A "whopper" is a huge, usually humorous, lie. Write an original whopper.

PURPOSE: Expressive

MODE: Narrative

CREATIVE THINKING SKILLS: Flexibility, originality, elaboration

EXTENSION: Tall tales are based on a series of "whoppers" about legendary heroes. Write a tall tale about such a hero. Include the whopper you wrote for the warm-up.

TEACHER NOTES/ COMMENTS:

WARM-UP TEN

WARM-UP:

What does a hurt feeling look like? Draw one and then write a description of it.

PURPOSE:

Informative

MODE:

Descriptive

CREATIVE THINKING SKILLS:

Flexibility, originality, elaboration

EXTENSION:

How do you think other feelings might look if we could see them? Choose some common emotions. Draw them and write descriptions of each one.

TEACHER NOTES/ COMMENTS:

WARM-UP ELEVEN

WARM-UP:	You have just seen a "dalumph" for the first time. What is it? How is it used?
PURPOSE:	Informative
MODE:	Descriptive
CREATIVE THINKING SKILLS:	Flexibility, originality, elaboration
EXTENSION:	Create several (8-10) nonsense words. Write dictionary entries for each of them. Include definitions, pronunciations, parts of speech, and a sentence for each.
TEACHER NOTES/ COMMENTS:	

WARM-UP TWELVE

WARM-UP: Write a sentence that has words that all begin with the same letter.

PURPOSE: Informative

MODE: Descriptive

CREATIVE THINKING SKILLS: Fluency, flexibility, originality

EXTENSION: "Tongue-twisters" are fun to say. Write several tongue-twisters about your school. Challenge your classmates to say them correctly - and fast.

TEACHER NOTES/ COMMENTS:

WARM-UP THIRTEEN

WARM-UP: Your bedroom is a mess. Write a warning sign to hang on your bedroom door.

PURPOSE: Informative

MODE: Descriptive

CREATIVE THINKING SKILLS: Flexibility, originality

EXTENSION: Write a humorous list of suggestions for keeping a bedroom clean. Present your list to your classmates as an oral presentation.

TEACHER NOTES/ COMMENTS:

WARM-UP FOURTEEN

WARM-UP: Think about the word yellow. What comes to mind? Make a list of your thoughts.

PURPOSE: Informative

MODE: Descriptive

CREATIVE THINKING SKILLS: Fluency, flexibility, elaboration

EXTENSION: Use your list of ideas from the warm-up to write metaphors about yellow. Begin each metaphor with "Yellow is. . ." Arrange your metaphors as a poem.

TEACHER NOTES/ COMMENTS:

WARM-UP FIFTEEN

WARM-UP: Write a list of reasons why students *should* have homework.

PURPOSE: Persuasive

MODE: Evaluative

CREATIVE THINKING SKILLS: Fluency, flexibility, originality

EXTENSION: Prepare a speech to present to your class titled "All Students Need Homework." Use the ideas you listed in the warm-up. Present your speech to the class.

TEACHER NOTES/ COMMENTS:

WARM-UP SIXTEEN

WARM-UP:	Write a list of reasons why students *should not* have homework.
PURPOSE:	Persuasive
MODE:	Evaluative
CREATIVE THINKING SKILLS:	Fluency, flexibility, originality
EXTENSION:	Prepare a speech to present to your class titled "Students Do Not Need Homework." Use the ideas you listed in the warm-up. Present your speech to the class.
TEACHER NOTES/ COMMENTS:	

WARM-UP SEVENTEEN

WARM-UP: What would you like to know about being a mother or father?

PURPOSE: Informative

MODE: Narrative

CREATIVE THINKING SKILLS: Flexibility, elaboration

EXTENSION: Rewrite your answers to the warm-up as a set of questions. Interview an adult who is a parent. Use the questions you wrote. What did you find out?

TEACHER NOTES/ COMMENTS:

WARM-UP EIGHTEEN

WARM-UP: How is your school like a baseball game?
Explain your comparison.

PURPOSE: Informative

MODE: Classificatory

**CREATIVE
THINKING SKILLS:** Flexibility, originality, elaboration

EXTENSION: What else is your school like? Write a poem
about your school. Begin each line with this
phrase: "School is like. . ." and end it
with ". . .because. . ."

**TEACHER NOTES/
COMMENTS:**

WARM-UP NINETEEN

WARM-UP:	You have probably received a remedy when you were ill. Write a remedy for sadness.
PURPOSE:	Informative
MODE:	Narrative
CREATIVE THINKING SKILLS:	Flexibility, originality, elaboration
EXTENSION:	There are many old folk remedies that many people believe. Interview several adults and ask what folk remedies they know or believe. Write them in a list.
TEACHER NOTES/ COMMENTS:	

WARM-UP TWENTY

WARM-UP:

Everyone is "bugged" by something. Make a list of things that bother you.

PURPOSE:

Expressive

MODE:

Descriptive

CREATIVE THINKING SKILLS:

Fluency, originality

EXTENSION:

Look at your list for the warm-up. Choose the one item on the list that bothers you most. Write a letter of complaint about it to "Dear Abby."

TEACHER NOTES/ COMMENTS:

WARM-UP TWENTY-ONE

WARM-UP: If you could star on a television program, which one would it be? Why?

PURPOSE: Persuasive

MODE: Descriptive

CREATIVE THINKING SKILLS: Flexibility, elaboration

EXTENSION: You are scheduled to appear on your favorite television program. Write an outline of the story's plot. Then decide who will star with you in the program.

TEACHER NOTES/ COMMENTS:

WARM-UP TWENTY-TWO

WARM-UP: Choose a picture from a magazine. Write a story based on the picture.

PURPOSE: Expressive

MODE: Narrative

CREATIVE THINKING SKILLS: Flexibility, originality, elaboration

EXTENSION: Now rewrite your story as a news article. How will the two pieces of writing differ? Which one was easier for you to write? Why?

TEACHER NOTES/ COMMENTS:

WARM-UP TWENTY-THREE

WARM-UP:	Think about your family's washing machine. How are you like the washing machine?
PURPOSE:	Expressive
MODE:	Classificatory
CREATIVE THINKING SKILLS:	Flexibility, originality, elaboration
EXTENSION:	Suppose you really were a washing machine. Write a list of complaints you would give to your owners and suggestions for improving your life.
TEACHER NOTES/ COMMENTS:	

WARM-UP:	You have a new job with a greeting card company. Write a greeting for a birthday card.
PURPOSE:	Expressive
MODE:	Descriptive
CREATIVE THINKING SKILLS:	Originality, elaboration
EXTENSION:	Now try your hand at other kinds of greetings. For example, write greetings for an anniversary card, a get well card, and a graduation card.
TEACHER NOTES/ COMMENTS:	

WARM-UP TWENTY-FIVE

WARM-UP:	You have been granted an interview with the president. Write the questions you'll ask.
PURPOSE:	Informative
MODE:	Narrative
CREATIVE THINKING SKILLS:	Flexibility, originality
EXTENSION:	Pretend there is really a chance to interview the president if your letter is chosen as the best request. Write the letter you would send to the president.
TEACHER NOTES/ COMMENTS:	

WARM-UP TWENTY-SIX

WARM-UP: Create happiness on your paper using symbols, words, pictures, phrases, etc.

PURPOSE: Informative

MODE: Descriptive

CREATIVE THINKING SKILLS: Fluency, flexibility, originality, elaboration

EXTENSION: Write a recipe for making happiness. Make sure you follow the regular pattern for writing a recipe, but use your creativity to make it unique.

TEACHER NOTES/ COMMENTS:

WARM-UP TWENTY-SEVEN

WARM-UP:	What are your three best qualities? Why do you think they are useful?
PURPOSE:	Informative
MODE:	Descriptive
CREATIVE THINKING SKILLS:	Flexibility, elaboration
EXTENSION:	Select a want ad from the paper that describes a job you would like to have. Write a letter to the employer explaining why you would be good for the job.
TEACHER NOTES/ COMMENTS:	

WARM-UP TWENTY-EIGHT

WARM-UP: You will have a test in your English class tomorrow. Write three questions for the test.

PURPOSE: Informative

MODE: Descriptive

CREATIVE THINKING SKILLS: Flexibility

EXTENSION: Create a test for your teacher. Decide with your teacher what the topic of the test will be. (Examples: current events, rock music)

TEACHER NOTES/ COMMENTS:

WARM-UP TWENTY-NINE

WARM-UP:	What is the best film you have seen lately? Write a review of the film.
PURPOSE:	Informative
MODE:	Descriptive
CREATIVE THINKING SKILLS:	Flexibility, originality, elaboration
EXTENSION:	You have written a review of the film. Now create an original advertisement for the film. Make sure your advertisement would influence others to see the film.
TEACHER NOTES/ COMMENTS:	

WARM-UP THIRTY

WARM-UP:	You're the local weatherman. What will the weather be tomorrow? Write the forecast.
PURPOSE:	Informative
MODE:	Descriptive
CREATIVE THINKING SKILLS:	Flexibility, originality, elaboration
EXTENSION:	Based upon your weather forecast, what would be a good way to spend the day tomorrow? Plan your day and make a list of the things you might do.
TEACHER NOTES/ COMMENTS:	

WARM-UP THIRTY-ONE

WARM-UP:	Would you rather be a cloud in the sky or the sun? Why?
PURPOSE:	Persuasive
MODE:	Classificatory
CREATIVE THINKING SKILLS:	Flexibility, originality, elaboration
EXTENSION:	Pretend you are either a cloud or the sun. Write a speech you might give to the people on Earth. Present your speech in class.
TEACHER NOTES/ COMMENTS:	

WARM-UP THIRTY-TWO

WARM-UP: Create a riddle that is based on numbers. Can your friend solve it?

PURPOSE: Informative

MODE: Descriptive

CREATIVE THINKING SKILLS: Originality, elaboration

EXTENSION: Create other riddles related to the other subjects you study in school. For example, write riddles for science, English, and social studies.

TEACHER NOTES/ COMMENTS:

WARM-UP THIRTY-THREE

WARM-UP: What is your favorite cereal? Design a label for a new cereal you would like to sell.

PURPOSE: Informative

MODE: Descriptive

CREATIVE THINKING SKILLS: Originality, elaboration

EXTENSION: Cover an old cereal box with white paper. Then design a box for your new cereal. Display your cereal box. How do others respond? Would they buy it?

TEACHER NOTES/ COMMENTS:

WARM-UP THIRTY-FOUR

WARM-UP:	Complete this sentence: If I could be a. . . I. . . Why?
PURPOSE:	Persuasive
MODE:	Descriptive
CREATIVE THINKING SKILLS:	Flexibility, originality, elaboration
EXTENSION:	Write a story titled "My Life As ________________ (idea from warm-up)." Make sure your story shows what your life is really like.
TEACHER NOTES/ COMMENTS:	

WARM-UP THIRTY-FIVE

WARM-UP:	It is your birthday. Plan the perfect menu for your birthday party.
PURPOSE:	Informative
MODE:	Descriptive
CREATIVE THINKING SKILLS:	Originality, elaboration
EXTENSION:	Now design the perfect invitation for your birthday party. Make sure your card includes all the important information and has an attractive design.
TEACHER NOTES/ COMMENTS:	

WARM-UP THIRTY-SIX

WARM-UP: Do you like to smile? Make a list of all the things that make you smile.

PURPOSE: Expressive

MODE: Descriptive

CREATIVE THINKING SKILLS: Fluency

EXTENSION: Write a poem about smiling. You may include the ideas you listed in your warm-up. Recite your poem for your classmates. Do the same things make people smile?`

TEACHER NOTES/ COMMENTS:

WARM-UP: You and your brother/sister just had an argument. Write the dialogue.

PURPOSE: Expressive

MODE: Narrative

CREATIVE THINKING SKILLS: Elaboration

EXTENSION: Prepare the dialogue as a small skit. Have a classmate perform the skit with you. Are you able to show the proper emotions as you perform?

TEACHER NOTES/ COMMENTS:

WARM-UP THIRTY-EIGHT

WARM-UP: Write a conversation a school bus and a school might have on a Monday morning.

PURPOSE: Expressive

MODE: Narrative

CREATIVE THINKING SKILLS: Flexibility, originality, elaboration

EXTENSION: Use your imaginary conversation as the basis for an original cartoon strip. Draw the cartoon strip with the proper dialogue. Display your cartoon in the classroom.

TEACHER NOTES/ COMMENTS:

WARM-UP THIRTY-NINE

WARM-UP: Write three questions that you hope no one ever asks you.

PURPOSE: Expressive

MODE: Descriptive

CREATIVE THINKING SKILLS: Flexibility, originality

EXTENSION: Write a paragraph that explains why you would not want to be asked one of the questions from the warm-up. Make sure you give a clear explanation of your reasons.

TEACHER NOTES/ COMMENTS:

WARM-UP FORTY

<table>
<tr><td>WARM-UP:</td><td>The headline about you said, "Famous Student Offers Advice." Write the article.</td></tr>
<tr><td>PURPOSE:</td><td>Informative</td></tr>
<tr><td>MODE:</td><td>Narrative</td></tr>
<tr><td>CREATIVE THINKING SKILLS:</td><td>Flexibility, originality, elaboration</td></tr>
<tr><td>EXTENSION:</td><td>How do people feel about the advice you offered? Write an editorial that expresses an opinion about the advice you gave. Then write a response to the editorial.</td></tr>
<tr><td>TEACHER NOTES/ COMMENTS:</td><td></td></tr>
</table>

WARM-UP FORTY-ONE

WARM-UP:	What will you eat for lunch today? Write an advertisement for your lunch.
PURPOSE:	Informative
MODE:	Descriptive
CREATIVE THINKING SKILLS:	Flexibility, originality
EXTENSION:	You wrote an advertisement for your lunch. Now create a picture ad to accompany it. Present your advertisements to your classmates.
TEACHER NOTES/ COMMENTS:	

WARM-UP FORTY-TWO

WARM-UP:

Write the first line of a mystery story. Now write the last line.

PURPOSE:

Expressive

MODE:

Narrative

CREATIVE THINKING SKILLS:

Flexibility, originality

EXTENSION:

Trade the first and last lines of your mystery for the first and last lines written by another student. Write the rest of the story for the new lines you have.

TEACHER NOTES/ COMMENTS:

WARM-UP FORTY-THREE

WARM-UP: You have a pen pal in Russia. Write a letter introducing yourself.

PURPOSE: Informative

MODE: Descriptive

CREATIVE THINKING SKILLS: Flexibility, elaboration

EXTENSION: You want your pen pal to understand your country. What five items would you send to help the person understand the USA? Describe and explain each choice.

TEACHER NOTES/ COMMENTS:

WARM-UP FORTY-FOUR

WARM-UP:	You are asked to create a new highway sign. What will its message be?
PURPOSE:	Informative
MODE:	Descriptive
CREATIVE THINKING SKILLS:	Flexibility, originality
EXTENSION:	Create a humorous road sign you would like to see on the road. Why do you think this sign would be a good addition to the signs we have now?
TEACHER NOTES/ COMMENTS:	

WARM-UP FORTY-FIVE

WARM-UP:	The answer is "tomorrow." Write five questions for this answer.
PURPOSE:	Informative
MODE:	Classificatory
CREATIVE THINKING SKILLS:	Fluency, flexibility, originality
EXTENSION:	Design a game similar to a television quiz show. What kind of questions will you ask the contestants? Have members of your class compete in the game.
TEACHER NOTES/ COMMENTS:	

WARM-UP FORTY-SIX

WARM-UP:

List three facts about yourself most people don't know, but you want them to know.

PURPOSE:

Informative

MODE:

Descriptive

CREATIVE THINKING SKILLS:

Fluency, flexibility, elaboration

EXTENSION:

Write a description of yourself, but do not include your name. Have the teacher read it to the class. How many people can identify you as the writer?

TEACHER NOTES/ COMMENTS:

WARM-UP FORTY-SEVEN

WARM-UP: Create a myth that explains something about your state's geography.

PURPOSE: Expressive

MODE: Narrative

CREATIVE THINKING SKILLS: Flexibility, originality, elaboration

EXTENSION: Rewrite your myth as a play. Design simple costumes and scenery. Perform the play for students in another class in your school.

TEACHER NOTES/ COMMENTS:

WARM-UP FORTY-EIGHT

WARM-UP: Write a conversation that a microscope and a bacterium might have.

PURPOSE: Expressive

MODE: Narrative

CREATIVE THINKING SKILLS: Flexibility, originality, elaboration

EXTENSION: Use the conversation between the microscope and bacterium as the basis for a cartoon strip. What will you name the characters? How will you draw them?

TEACHER NOTES/ COMMENTS:

WARM-UP FORTY-NINE

WARM-UP: What are the best qualities of the place where you live?

PURPOSE: Informative

MODE: Descriptive

CREATIVE THINKING SKILLS: Fluency, elaboration

EXTENSION: Create a travel brochure to attract tourists to the place you live. What would interest people? Include pictures and descriptive words in the brochure.

TEACHER NOTES/ COMMENTS:

WARM-UP FIFTY

WARM-UP: Retell a fairy tale as if it happened in your neighborhood.

PURPOSE: Expressive

MODE: Narrative

CREATIVE THINKING SKILLS: Flexibility, originality, elaboration

EXTENSION: Think of one character from two different fairy tales. What would happen if they met each other? What would they say? Write the conversation they might have.

TEACHER NOTES/ COMMENTS:

WARM-UP FIFTY-ONE

WARM-UP: George Washington will visit your class. Write an appropriate introduction for him.

PURPOSE: Informative

MODE: Descriptive

CREATIVE THINKING SKILLS: Flexibility, originality, elaboration

EXTENSION: If George Washington did visit your class, what would you want to ask him? Write a list of questions you would use when interviewing him.

TEACHER NOTES/ COMMENTS:

WARM-UP FIFTY-TWO

WARM-UP: Create a list of health rules students of your age should follow.

PURPOSE: Informative

MODE: Narrative

CREATIVE THINKING SKILLS: Fluency, flexibility, originality

EXTENSION: What is the number one health problem for students your age? Research and find out. Then write a report on this health problem.

TEACHER NOTES/ COMMENTS:

WARM-UP FIFTY-THREE

WARM-UP: Punctuation rules can be difficult to learn and follow. What would happen if we had no rules?

PURPOSE: Informative

MODE: Narrative

CREATIVE THINKING SKILLS: Flexibility, originality, elaboration

EXTENSION: Select a paragraph from one of your textbooks. Rewrite it, but omit all the punctuation. Give the rewritten paragraph to a friend to read. Will s/he have problems?

TEACHER NOTES/ COMMENTS:

WARM-UP FIFTY-FOUR

WARM-UP: Would you rather be a verb or a noun? Explain your choice.

PURPOSE: Persuasive

MODE: Classificatory

CREATIVE THINKING SKILLS: Flexibility, originality, elaboration

EXTENSION: Imagine our language had no verbs. What would that be like? What problems would we have in communicating? What if we had verbs, but no nouns?

TEACHER NOTES/ COMMENTS:

WARM-UP FIFTY-FIVE

WARM-UP:	Write a job description or a want ad for the position you want to play in a sport.
PURPOSE:	Informative
MODE:	Descriptive
CREATIVE THINKING SKILLS:	Flexibility, elaboration
EXTENSION:	Pretend you could write a letter of application for this position on a team. Write the letter you would submit to the coach.
TEACHER NOTES/ COMMENTS:	

WARM-UP FIFTY-SIX

WARM-UP: List 5-10 interesting facts you have learned recently in science class.

PURPOSE: Informative

MODE: Descriptive

CREATIVE THINKING SKILLS: Fluency

EXTENSION: Use the facts you listed in the warm-up as the basis for a science fiction story. Who will the characters be? What will happen to them?

TEACHER NOTES/ COMMENTS:

WARM-UP FIFTY-SEVEN

WARM-UP: Write directions for solving a math problem you recently solved in math class.

PURPOSE: Informative

MODE: Narrative

CREATIVE THINKING SKILLS: Flexibility, elaboration

EXTENSION: Is it easy or difficult to write an explanation for solving a math problem? Explain what makes it easy or difficult for you.

TEACHER NOTES/ COMMENTS:

WARM-UP FIFTY-EIGHT

WARM-UP: Create a song or jingle to help you remember a difficult concept from English class.

PURPOSE: Informative

MODE: Descriptive

CREATIVE THINKING SKILLS: Flexibility, originality, elaboration

EXTENSION: Are you brave enough to sing your song or jingle for the class? If you are not, at least read the words to them. Would it help them remember?

TEACHER NOTES/ COMMENTS:

WARM-UP FIFTY-NINE

WARM-UP: Complete this sentence: I always feel happier when I see. . . because. . .

PURPOSE: Expressive

MODE: Descriptive

CREATIVE THINKING SKILLS: Fluency, elaboration

EXTENSION: Write a poem entitled "Happiness Is. . .". Begin each line of the poem with the words "Happiness is. . ." Read your poem to the class.

TEACHER NOTES/ COMMENTS:

WARM-UP SIXTY

WARM-UP: Create a new dessert. Write the recipe for this new creation.

PURPOSE: Informative

MODE: Narrative

CREATIVE THINKING SKILLS: Flexibility, originality, elaboration

EXTENSION: Write a description of your new dessert. Your description will appear on the packaging of the dessert. How will you write this description?

TEACHER NOTES/ COMMENTS:

WARM-UP SIXTY-ONE

WARM-UP: Suppose you had been King Midas. How would you have used your "golden touch?"

PURPOSE: Expressive

MODE: Narrative

CREATIVE THINKING SKILLS: Flexibility, originality, elaboration

EXTENSION: Imagine you have been given a special "touch" - the "peanut butter touch." Write a story about an adventure you have as the main character, "King Sticky."

TEACHER NOTES/ COMMENTS:

WARM-UP SIXTY-TWO

WARM-UP: Would you rather be the sun or the moon?
Explain your choice.

PURPOSE: Persuasive

MODE: Classificatory

**CREATIVE
THINKING SKILLS:**   Flexibility, originality, elaboration

EXTENSION: Find a legend or myth about the sun or moon.
Rewrite the legend or myth as if it were happen-
ing today. How would the story change?

**TEACHER NOTES/
COMMENTS:**

WARM-UP: You are an Olympic champion. How does it feel? What was most exciting?

PURPOSE: Expressive

MODE: Descriptive

CREATIVE THINKING SKILLS: Flexibility, originality, elaboration

EXTENSION: Write a news article about your Olympic victory. Include the important facts. Make sure your story has a headline, dateline, and other parts of a news item.

TEACHER NOTES/ COMMENTS:

WARM-UP SIXTY-FOUR

WARM-UP: Complete this sentence:
A coffee mug is like a cookie. . . because. . .

PURPOSE: Informative

MODE: Classificatory

CREATIVE THINKING SKILLS: Flexibility, originality, elaboration

EXTENSION: The sentence you completed in the warm-up is a simile. Write some original similes comparing the items in a classroom to different kinds of animals.

TEACHER NOTES/ COMMENTS:

WARM-UP SIXTY-FIVE

WARM-UP: Complete this thought:
If I had three wishes, I would surely. . .

PURPOSE: Expressive

MODE: Narrative

CREATIVE THINKING SKILLS: Flexibility, originality, elaboration

EXTENSION: Many fairy tales are based on the making and granting of wishes. Write an original fairy tale about a special wish. Write the story for a young child.

TEACHER NOTES/ COMMENTS:

WARM-UP SIXTY-SIX

WARM-UP:	How could you use a bicycle to improve a vending machine? Explain your answer.
PURPOSE:	Informative
MODE:	Narrative
CREATIVE THINKING SKILLS:	Flexibility, originality, elaboration
EXTENSION:	Draw a diagram of your new invention. Name it and label all of its parts. Write a description of it that would appear with the diagram in a catalog.
TEACHER NOTES/ COMMENTS:	

WARM-UP SIXTY-SEVEN

WARM-UP: Create loneliness on your paper with symbols, words, phrases, pictures, etc.

PURPOSE: Expressive

MODE: Descriptive

CREATIVE THINKING SKILLS: Fluency, flexibility, originality, elaboration

EXTENSION: Write an original poem about loneliness. Use the ideas you generated in the warm-up. How does your poem compare to what other poets say about loneliness?

TEACHER NOTES/ COMMENTS:

WARM-UP SIXTY-EIGHT

WARM-UP: You have won the lead in a Broadway play. Describe your role and costume(s).

PURPOSE: Informative

MODE: Descriptive

CREATIVE THINKING SKILLS: Flexibility, originality, elaboration

EXTENSION: You have given your first performance and the reviews are in. What did the best and worst reviews say about your performance?

TEACHER NOTES/ COMMENTS:

WARM-UP SIXTY-NINE

WARM-UP: Complete this thought:
I feel students should never have to. . .
because. . .

PURPOSE: Persuasive

MODE: Evaluative

**CREATIVE
THINKING SKILLS:** Flexibility, originality, elaboration

EXTENSION: Write an editorial for your school newspaper
explaining why you feel students shouldn't
have to do a certain activity (see warm-up).

**TEACHER NOTES/
COMMENTS:**

WARM-UP SEVENTY

WARM-UP: Explain why you believe your birthday should be the next national holiday.

PURPOSE: Persuasive

MODE: Evaluative

CREATIVE THINKING SKILLS: Flexibility, originality, elaboration

EXTENSION: Your birthday has been named a national holiday. Describe how people should celebrate the new holiday. (Think about how we celebrate other holidays.)

TEACHER NOTES/ COMMENTS:

WARM-UP SEVENTY-ONE

WARM-UP:	Would you rather be a carpet or a doorbell? Explain your choice.
PURPOSE:	Persuasive
MODE:	Classificatory
CREATIVE THINKING SKILLS:	Flexibility, originality, elaboration
EXTENSION:	Doorbells ring to let us know someone is at the door. Create a new device for alerting us. Write a description of it and explain why it's better than a bell.
TEACHER NOTES/ COMMENTS:	

WARM-UP SEVENTY-TWO

WARM-UP:	It seems like many people are sad. Write a prescription for curing sadness.
PURPOSE:	Informative
MODE:	Narrative
CREATIVE THINKING SKILLS:	Flexibility, originality, elaboration
EXTENSION:	The headline reads "Student Inventor Finds Cure For Sadness." Write the story that accompanies the article.
TEACHER NOTES/ COMMENTS:	